LADYBUG FOUNDATION
CHARITIES STARTED BY KIDS!
BY MELISSA SHERMAN PEARL

Published in the United States of America by Cherry Lake Publishing
Ann Arbor, Michigan
www.cherrylakepublishing.com

Reading Adviser: Marla Conn MS, Ed., Literacy specialist, Read-Ability, Inc.

Photo Credits: © Photo used with permission from the Ladybug Foundation, cover, 11, 19, 21;
© Stavrida/Shutterstock Images, 5; © Monkey Business Images/Shutterstock Images, 7;
© BestPhotoStudio/Shutterstock Images, 9; © wavebreakmedia/Shutterstock Images, 13;
© Rawpixel.com/Shutterstock Images, 15; © Michael Chamberlin/Shutterstock Images, 17

Copyright ©2018 by Cherry Lake Publishing
All rights reserved. No part of this book may be reproduced or utilized in any form
or by any means without written permission from the publisher.

LIBRARY OF CONGRESS CATALOGING-IN-PUBLICATION DATA HAS BEEN FILED AND IS AVAILABLE AT CATALOG.LOC.GOV

Names: Pearl, Melissa Sherman, author.
Title: Ladybug Foundation : charities started by kids! / by Melissa Sherman Pearl.
Description: Ann Arbor : Cherry Lake Publishing, [2018] |
    Series: How do they help? | Audience: Grade 4 to 6. |
    Includes bibliographical references and index.
Identifiers: LCCN 2017035927| ISBN 9781534107304 (hardcover) |
    ISBN 9781534109285 (pdf) | ISBN 9781534108295 (pbk.) |
    ISBN 9781534120273 (hosted ebook)
Subjects: LCSH: Ladybug Foundation—Juvenile literature. |
    Homelessness—Canada—Juvenile literature.
Classification: LCC HV4509 .P4294 2018 | DDC 362.5/9280971—dc23
    LC record available at https://lccn.loc.gov/2017035927

Cherry Lake Publishing would like to acknowledge the
work of The Partnership for 21st Century Learning. Please
visit *www.p21.org* for more information.

Printed in the United States of America
Corporate Graphics

CONTENTS

4 Seeing the World Around Her

10 Knowledge Is Empowerment

16 A Little Ladybug with Big, Strong Wings

22 Glossary

23 Find Out More

24 Index

24 About the Author

HOW DO THEY HELP?

SEEING THE WORLD AROUND HER

People who are homeless may sleep in hotels, shelters, or even on city sidewalks or park benches. They often don't get to eat on a regular basis. Canada's Ladybug Foundation raises funds for homeless shelters while spreading awareness about homelessness, hunger, and **poverty**.

When Hannah Taylor was 5 years old, she saw a man searching through

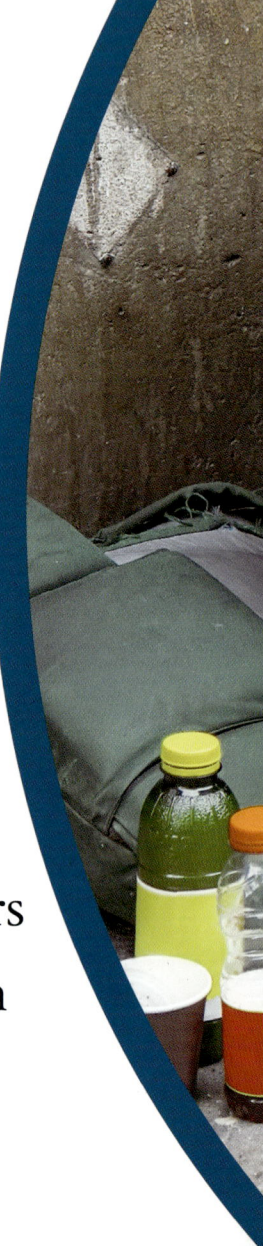

About 13% of Canadians aren't able to get enough healthy food to feed their families.

THINK!

Knowing her voice was just as important as a grown-up's, Hannah made calls to everyone she thought could help. Think about something that is important to you. Who would you call to help and why?

5

the trash for food. Nearly a year later, she was still worried about him. Her mom offered Hannah some **sage** advice. She said that Hannah might try and do something about it, and then "your heart won't feel so sad."

The next day, Hannah talked to her class about doing something to help. They decided to hold a bake and art sale. The money raised was donated to a local mission in Winnipeg, Canada. For Hannah's second fund-raiser, she and some

Bake sales are a popular way for schools and organizations to raise money.

THINK!

For Hannah, it was important to bring people together to work toward a common goal. Do you prefer to work in groups or by yourself?

volunteers made and **distributed** 5,000 jars painted like ladybugs to collect spare change.

Her next fund-raiser was selling cozy, red fleece Ladybug Scarves. Winnipeg can get awfully cold. These scarves would help the homeless stay warm through the winter.

To Hannah, a nice, warm scarf on a cold morning felt like a hug.

KNOWLEDGE IS EMPOWERMENT

Hannah continued to learn as much as she could. She spoke with anyone who'd listen about making a difference in the lives of the **impoverished**. She noticed that many don't see those who are homeless as people. "Instead of just seeing a problem," she thought, "we need to see human beings who need help." She also learned that

As Hannah learned more, she realized that the reasons for homelessness were more complex than she thought.

MAKE A GUESS!

Of the following, which do you think are factors in homelessness: poverty, lack of affordable housing, **inadequate** physical or mental health care, or family breakdown? The answer is, they can all lead to homelessness.

there isn't one main reason for poverty or homelessness.

    This **determined** young girl couldn't keep her thoughts to herself. She knew her voice was just as important and **profound** as a grown-up's. She decided to reach out to the "big bosses" in society and government.

    She asked her dad to help make a list of those big bosses. She phoned to invite them to lunch to talk about how they could help those in need.

Business and community leaders are often able to help support charity organizations.

They all said yes. After one of many meetings with individual leaders, Hannah realized that getting everyone together for a "Big Boss Lunch" would be more effective. One person can make a difference, but together they could actually make a change!

Hannah knew that it was good to get a lot of people involved with the Ladybug Foundation.

LOOK!

Why did Hannah choose to name her foundation after ladybugs? Ladybugs are thought to bring good luck, and she felt that the homeless, as well as the foundation, could use a little luck. Find out what else ladybugs are known for by searching online or at your local library.

15

A LITTLE LADYBUG WITH BIG, STRONG WINGS

Thanks to these lunches, Hannah developed relationships with powerful people who were happy to help. By the time she was 8, the Ladybug Foundation was a registered charitable organization in Canada.

Hannah continued raising money. She also started speaking to large groups of kids and grown-ups about how they could help people.

Hannah spoke to local schools about helping those affected by poverty.

As college graduation nears, Hannah maintains the two volunteer-run charities she founded. The Ladybug Foundation has supported more than 70 shelters, food banks, and soup kitchens and has raised more than $4 million. Her second organization is called makeChange: The Ladybug Foundation Education Program. makeChange involves **innovative** lesson plans that are taught in kindergarten through high school. This educational program was

Hannah plans to go to law school. She wants to study human rights law.

ASK QUESTIONS!

Hannah's top advice for young people hoping to make a difference is to learn as much as you can about what you care about. Why do you think knowledge is so powerful? Talk to your friends and family and see what they think.

developed to empower young people to get involved and make a change in the world—and it embraces everything that Hannah celebrates.

In September 2017, Hannah won a Muhammad Ali Humanitarian Award for her work with the homeless.

CREATE!

For one of Hannah's first fund-raisers, she painted baby food jars to look like ladybugs. These jars were used to collect coins. Paint a clean jar to represent your favorite charity, then collect coins and donate the funds.

GLOSSARY

determined (dih-TUR-mihnd) having a strong feeling and making a decision

distributed (dis-TRIB-yoot-id) gave things out to a number of people

impoverished (im-PAHV-rishd) poor or reduced to poverty

inadequate (in-AD-ih-kwit) in short supply

innovative (IN-uh-vay-tiv) introducing new methods or creative thinking

poverty (PAH-vur-tee) having little or no money for basic needs like food and shelter

profound (pruh-FOUND) very deep or moving

sage (SAYJ) wise and with good judgment

FIND OUT MORE

WEB SITES

www.ladybugfoundation.ca
Learn more about Hannah Taylor and her Ladybug Foundation.

www.ladybugeducation.ca
Learn more about makeChange: The Ladybug Foundation Education Program.

www.freespirit.com/pages/resource.cfm?file=1923
Read A Kids' Guide to Hunger & Homelessness: How to Take Action!

INDEX

"Big Boss Lunch," 14, 16

educational programs, 18–20
empowerment, 10–14, 20

families, breakdown of, 11
fund-raisers, 6–9, 16, 21

health care, 11
homelessness, 4, 10
　causes of, 11–12
housing, affordable, 11
hunger, 4

knowledge, 10–14, 19

Ladybug Foundation
　beginning of, 16
　impact of, 18
　what it is, 4–9
ladybugs, 8, 15, 21
lesson plans, 18–20
luck, 15

makeChange, 18–20

poverty, 4, 11, 12

Taylor, Hannah, 4–9, 10–14, 16
　advice for young people, 19
　early fund-raisers, 6–8, 21
　reaches out to "big bosses," 12–16

ABOUT THE AUTHOR

Melissa Sherman Pearl is a mother of two girls who understands and appreciates that you don't have to be an adult to make a difference.